BODIAM CASTLE

East Sussex

THE NATIONAL TRUST

The text of this guidebook has been written by David
Thackray, Archaeological Adviser to the National Trust.
For their help in various ways we would like to thank
Peregrine Bryant, Paul Everson, Mark Gardiner, Jim Past
and Philip Sinton.

Photographs: British Museum pages 11, 24, 25, 26, 35, 44, 48,
61, back cover; Kentish Studies Library, Maidstone page 9;
National Portrait Gallery page 8; National Trust Photographic
Library/Alasdair Ogilvie pages 4, 10, 15, 16, 17, 18, 20,
33, 36, 37, 38, 40, 41, 45, 46, 47, 49, 50, 51, 53, 55, 57;
NTPL/Unichrome page 6; NTPL/Don Carr front cover;
Newbery Smith Associates page 27; Royal Commission on the
Historical Monuments of England page 56; Victoria & Albert
Museum page 23 (left).

First published in Great Britain in 1991 by the National Trust
© 1991 The National Trust; reprinted 1995, 1999, 2001, 2004, 2007, 2008
Revised 2003
Registered charity no. 205846

ISBN 978-1-84359-090-3

Designed by James Shurmer

Phototypeset in Monotype Bembo Series 270
by Intraspan Limited, Smallfield, Surrey (s8030)

Colour reproduction by Acculith 76, Barnet, Hertfordshire

Printed by Hawthornes
for National Trust (Enterprises) Ltd, Heelis, Kemble Drive,
Swindon, Wilts SN2 2NA
on stock made from 75% recycled fibre

CONTENTS

INTRODUCTION

The impressive and beautiful symmetry of Bodiam Castle, with its massive towers and broad moat, appears the very epitome of the medieval castle. Yet it was constructed late in the history of castle building, at a time when the nobility were looking for comfortable residences, agreeable places to live in, outwardly ostentatious as expressions of their rank and status, yet incorporating the latest in military architecture: 'castles of chivalry'. Bodiam represents an evolutionary stage half-way between the austere fortresses of earlier centuries and the comfortable country mansions of the Tudor and Elizabethan periods.

Sir Edward Dalyngrigge, its builder, had amassed considerable wealth and status in the wars against France during the latter part of the fourteenth century, and in his services to the court and parliament at home. The wars persisted and the threat of a French invasion of the south coast from the Channel was a fear. Not surprisingly, therefore, Sir Edward claimed his castle would be of value in the event of invasion when he applied for a 'licence to crenellate' in 1385 – as indeed it might have been, at least against small raiding parties. He chose a site in the valley of the River Rother overlooking the wharves on the river frontage adjacent to Bodiam Bridge. A port for the export of Sussex iron may have been in existence here since Roman times, as the Roman road between Hastings and Rochester crossed the river at this point, with a substantial settlement on the south side of the river where tiles bearing the stamped impression of the *Classis Britannica*, the Roman Fleet, have been found. The siting of the castle does seem to demonstrate some strategic intent. However, a recent survey has suggested that the series of artificial ponds, which once adjoined the moat, were part of a carefully contrived landscape that had little military value, but was intended to enhance the setting of the castle and the status of its owner.

Whether meant as fortress or status symbol, Bodiam was soon overtaken by changes in military technology and domestic life. It was partially dismantled during the Civil War and endured several centuries of benign neglect. During the eighteenth century, as the ivy grew over the crumbling battlements, Bodiam was gradually transformed from an awkward anachronism into a romantic reminder of England's past, and numerous artists came to record it. In the nineteenth century the first active steps were taken to repair the monument by John Fuller and Lord Ashcombe, and later by Lord Curzon, who left it to the National Trust after his death in 1925.

(Opposite page) The entrance to the Gatehouse

Bodiam from the south-east

CHAPTER ONE
THE WARS WITH FRANCE

To understand why Sir Edward Dalyngrigge decided to build Bodiam Castle in 1385, one must look back fifty years to the beginning of the Hundred Years War. In 1337 the 25-year-old Edward III, already lord of the Duchy of Guyenne in south-west France, laid claim to the French Crown, considering that his mother, Isabel, the sister of the three previous Valois kings of France, had been wrongly disinherited by her cousin, Philip VI. For the next hundred years this family conflict was fought out with a mixture of chivalry and savagery that is described most vividly in the contemporary *Chronicles* of Froissart. French and English lords, speaking the same dialect of Anglo-Norman French, fought one another with honour and civility; their subjects were butchered unmercifully.

Control of the Channel was important from the outset. Portsmouth and Southampton were raided by the French in 1338, followed by Dover and Folkestone in 1339. According to Froissart, when King Edward heard that his flagship, the *Christopher*, had been captured by the French, he retorted, 'I have long wanted to fight them. We will do so, if it pleases God and St George. They have inflicted so much damage on me that I mean to settle accounts with them if I can.' In 1340, at the head of

The Battle of Crécy, as illustrated in Froissart's 'Chronicles'

his fleet, Edward sailed into Sluys harbour and destroyed the French fleet while it lay at anchor, giving the English command of the Channel for the next few years.

In 1346 Edward invaded Normandy and marched on Paris, leaving a trail of destruction behind him. On the battlefield of Crécy, north of the Somme, Edward's longbowmen defeated a much larger force of French cavalry under Philip VI, before moving on to blockade Calais, which was finally captured after almost a year's siege in 1347.

The following decade was one of intermittent warfare, for both countries had been weakened by the war and the Black Death of 1348–9. Edward III, however, was still far from satisfied. He had had notable victories, captured Calais, but lost the support of Flanders. Above all, he still had not won the Crown of France. Edward clearly wanted to renew the war and his eldest son, the Black Prince, who was not to be denied his share of the glory and the profits, was appointed Lieutenant in Gascony, where he went with a small army in 1355. After raiding and ravaging the Mediterranean provinces, the Black Prince marched north to reach the Loire in 1356 on a campaign of devastation in central and north-west France. A further notable victory was won by the Black Prince over Philip VI's son and successor, John, at the Battle of Poitiers. 'There died that day,' Froissart wrote, 'the finest flower of French chivalry.' King John found himself fighting with only his 14-year-old son Philip by his side and was forced to surrender. 'That evening the Prince of Wales gave a supper for the King of France and most of the captured counts and barons ... He himself served in all humility both at the King's table and at others, steadfastly refusing to sit down with the King despite all his entreaties. He insisted that he was not yet worthy to sit at the table of so mighty a prince and so brave a soldier as he had proved himself to be on that day.'

Edward III made a great effort to try to finish the war in a winter campaign of 1359–60, but things went against him and he lost the support of Navarre and the control of Burgundy. There was again further French privateering in the Channel, and the town of Rye on the Sussex coast was raided. However, Edward III still held King John in

Edward III, whose claim to the throne of France led to the Hundred Years War. 'His like had not been seen since the days of King Arthur' (Froissart). His tomb effigy is in Westminster Abbey

captivity and was able to negotiate a truce at Brétigny in 1360. The terms of the treaty, in which Edward renounced the claim to the Crown of France whilst retaining Aquitaine, Calais and other important provinces, in return for the freedom of the remainder of France and the release of King John for a substantial ransom, were never wholly fulfilled. Edward was unable, in particular, to evacuate English forces from the remainder of France and to prevent them from continuing to prey on the French.

This was the era of the 'Free Companies', private mercenary armies, nominally under the control of their King, but in reality selling their services to the highest bidder. Led by men such as Sir Robert Knollys, whose shield of arms is carved in relief on the Postern Gate at Bodiam, they indulged in looting and destruction on an appalling scale. The peasants of the Loire valley are said to have thrown themselves into the river in dread at the mere mention of Knollys's name. The charred gables of the towns through which his forces passed were known as 'Knollys's mitres'. The rewards of such plundering could be vast: in 1358 Knollys is said to have made 100,000 gold crowns and from his castle at Derval in Picardy he ruled as absolute master of the surrounding region.

Edward Dalyngrigge was one of many English soldiers who followed Knollys to France in search of

similar wealth and power. In 1367 he crossed the Channel with Edward III's second son, Lionel, Duke of Clarence, and he also fought under the banner of Richard Fitz-Alan, Earl of Arundel, whose patronage he was to enjoy for some twenty years. But it was under Sir Robert Knollys, who fought mainly in Normandy, Brittany and Picardy, that he was to make the fortune that enabled him to build Bodiam Castle.

Thanks in part to the freelance warfare of men like Dalyngrigge, intermittent fighting continued throughout the 1360s, although these were nominally years of peace. The Black Prince, who had been made ruler of Gascony, carried the war into Spain. In 1369 Edward III again renewed his claim to the Crown of France and open war recommenced. The French began to regain much that had been taken by the English. In the same year they burned Portsmouth and gradually assumed control of the Channel. A two-year truce was made at the Treaty of Bruges in 1375, which left Edward III with only Calais and a strip of coast from Bordeaux to Bayonne in south-west France, and gave the French fleet effective control of the Channel for the next fifteen years.

In 1376 the Black Prince, Froissart's 'most gallant man and chivalrous prince', died, having returned to England in ill-health. The following year Edward III also died and his young grandson Richard II

Cooling Castle near Rochester, which, like Bodiam, was built in the 1380s in response to the threat of French invasion

Bodiam Castle from the north-west

succeeded to the throne. The Truce of Bruges expired and the French began attacks on the south coast again. Only ten days after Edward III's death a French fleet under Admiral Jean de Vienne attacked and burnt Rye and Hastings and made assaults on the Isle of Wight. The attacks were not entirely one-sided; the church bells of Rye, stolen by the French in the attack in 1377, were recaptured by the men of Rye in a return raid the following year. However, the south coast was clearly vulnerable and efforts had to be made to increase its defences.

Money was voted by Parliament for the defence of the south coast; indeed work on a number of important castles and other defences had already been carried out. The now-vanished castle over-looking the Medway at Queenborough in Kent was built as a royal castle in the 1360s, and about the same time the defences of Southampton were strengthened. By 1379, the threat of a French invasion was imminent and further defence works

were initiated in Kent. In 1380 the royal master-mason Henry Yevele began building the West Gate of Canterbury for Archbishop Simon Sudbury, and the city was further fortified. In 1381, a licence to fortify and crenellate Cooling Castle near Rochester was granted to John of Cobham, like Dalyngrigge one of Knollys's lieutenants.

The threat of invasion intensified still further following the failure of Bishop Despenser's ex-pedition to Flanders in 1383. In 1385 a French invasion fleet of 1,200 cogs (broad-beamed ships), galleys and barges gathered at Sluys, throwing the whole of southern England into panic. Thousands were said to have gone on a spending spree, hoarding provisions as though invasion and defeat by the French were only days away. The French fleet did not sail that summer because of the illness of Philip the Bold, Duke of Burgundy, but it was not surprising that in the atmosphere which prevailed throughout the autumn of 1385 Edward Dalyn-grigge should have been given a licence to fortify his manor house at Bodiam.

CHAPTER TWO

SIR EDWARD DALYNGRIGGE

Sir Edward Dalyngrigge already belonged to an old-established Sussex family, from Dalling Ridge near East Grinstead, but he returned from fighting in France in 1377 immensely more wealthy and powerful. Having married Elizabeth, heiress of the family of Wardedieu or Wardeux, who had held the manor of Bodiam since before 1330, Sir Edward was in possession of the manor by 1378. Through his wife Sir Edward acquired a moated manor house, which lay just to the north of Bodiam church in the adjacent valley of the Kent Ditch. From

within this moated site the traces of a medieval timber-framed hall were excavated in the 1960s and 1970s. The finds, particularly the pottery, from the excavations of this building show that it was occupied from the late thirteenth century and throughout the fourteenth century, falling into disuse at approximately the time when the castle was built.

A second possible site of a late thirteenth-century house was hinted at by excavation in the 1960s. It was built on an artificial terrace, known at least since the early eighteenth century as the 'Gun Garden', on

Bodiam church from the south-west; watercolour by S. H. Grimm, 1784 (British Museum). The moated manor house which Sir Edward had acquired by 1378 (now gone) lay just to the north

the hill north of and overlooking the castle itself (see Chapter Seven). It has been suggested, therefore, that these two houses, both possibly of manorial status, were the houses of two branches of the Wardedieu family. The Wardedieus had themselves acquired the manor by marriage from the de Bodeham family, who had held it since the Norman Conquest, when it was granted to Hugh of Eu, whose son first took the title 'de Bodeham' from the name of the Saxon settlement on the site. Dalyngrigge may have resided in one or other of these houses until the castle was completed, although his estates included another house at Bolebrook, near Hartfield in East Sussex.

Dalyngrigge was Knight of the Shire for Sussex in ten parliaments between 1379 and 1388 and was, without doubt, one of the most influential of the Sussex gentry at this time. In 1380 he was made a member of the Commission considering the state of the realm and the possessions, expenses and revenues of the royal household. In the same year he was appointed to survey Winchelsea and to consider how the town should be fortified against the French. Although Bodiam was about 14 miles up the River Rother from Rye and slightly further from Winchelsea, it was still regarded as part of the port of Winchelsea; a fact that clearly influenced Sir Edward in his choice of site for the castle. His

'King Richard in great danger in the City of London and the rebels discomfited', from Froissart's 'Chronicles'. Dalyngrigge helped to put down the Peasants' Revolt in 1381

concern over the defence of the coast is again demonstrated in 1384–5, when he is recorded as a member of a Commission called to fortify the nearby port of Rye.

The threat from a foreign invader was a pressing enough reason for building a well-defended castle close to the south coast, but Sir Edward also had cause to be concerned by internal threats. In 1381 peasants from Kent, Essex, Sussex and Bedfordshire rose in revolt. They destroyed many manor houses on their march to London, overran the Tower of London and hacked off the head of Archbishop Sudbury. The ferocity with which the Peasants' Revolt was ultimately put down by Richard II's supporters, who included Knollys and Dalyngrigge, left a legacy of continuing popular unrest in the south-eastern counties: for example, in 1383 the Earl of Arundel's castle at Lewes was stormed and pillaged.

In the same year Sir Edward obtained a royal grant to hold a weekly market at his manor of Bodiam and an annual fair on 25 and 26 May, the vigil and feast day of St Augustine.

In 1384 the King's uncle, John of Gaunt, Duke of Lancaster, took out a lawsuit against Dalyngrigge to try to restrain him from interference with the Duke's recently acquired Sussex estates. Resentment of the powerful Duke of Lancaster and his estates was felt by many of the Sussex gentry, and Dalyngrigge was essentially representing their grievances. There was also considerable strength of feeling against the Duke from the villagers on his estates. Dalyngrigge's behaviour in court, where he appeared in his own defence, was violent and unruly and gives a good indication of his personality. Twice during the proceedings Sir Edward threw down the gauntlet in court. His action, hardly appropriate for the charges of trespass and illegal hunting laid against him, was more reminiscent of the court of chivalry, and implied that he saw the case more as a matter of honour than of legality. His concern was fundamentally that his local standing was threatened by John of Gaunt's acquisition and authority over neighbouring estates. John of Gaunt won his lawsuit, but Dalyngrigge suffered little harm as a result; his patron, the Earl of Arundel, interceded for him with the King, and despite Lan-

caster's immediate displeasure, Dalyngrigge was returned to the Parliament in Westminster soon after. John of Gaunt could not afford for too long to set himself against a man of Dalyngrigge's local status.

Just a year later, in October 1385, Dalyngrigge received a Royal licence to:

Strengthen with a wall of stone and lime, and crenellate and, construct and make into a Castle his manor house Bodyham, near the sea, in the county of Sussex, for defence of the adjacent country, and, resistance to our enemies.

In the same year that Sir Edward received the licence to crenellate (translated in full in the Appendix), he was granted a royal licence to divert a watercourse from 'Dalyngreggesbay', upstream in Salehurst, to Bodiam to power a watermill. The mill was situated south of the castle between it and the river, fed by the large mill-pond, the earthwork banks of which have been known since Lord Curzon's time as the 'Tiltyard' (see Chapter Seven). It is unlikely that Dalyngrigge himself was present to oversee the first stages in building Bodiam. For between 1386–7 he was appointed Captain of the French port of Brest.

By 1390 the threat of war with France had receded. Sir Edward was appointed to several commissions – to conclude a truce with the King of France, to make conditions with the Earl of Flanders and with the people of Ghent, Bruges and Ypres, and to survey the castles and fortresses of Calais and Picardy. In 1390 he was one of nine knights who attached their seal to a letter sent to the Pope deploring the excesses of the Church. Sir Edward's status in the country was further reflected in 1392 when he was appointed by the King as Keeper of the Tower of London and Governor of the City following a dispute between the King and the Mayor and officers of the City of London. By this time the castle must have been completed, but Sir Edward was not to enjoy it for long. He died some time before 1395 and was succeeded by his son, Sir John Dalyngrigge.

CHAPTER THREE
BODIAM: A STRONGHOLD AND A RESIDENCE

The licence to crenellate empowered Sir Edward Dalyngrigge to fortify with a wall and battlements his manor house at Bodiam. However, this is not apparently what he did. He selected a new site, on a slightly elevated position with a view commanding a bridge (recorded as early as 1313) and the important wharves on the River Rother. This strategic site would give the defender the upper hand over bands of French raiders coming up the river. To that extent Bodiam was an element in the defence of the south coast behind the Cinque Ports. Following the granting of the licence, the castle must have been completed within a fairly short time, as it is, with very few exceptions, the work of one episode of building in one style and in local Wealden sandstone. Given the French threat to the south coast, speed was clearly essential.

The building of Bodiam Castle comes late in the history of English castles. It is unlike many earlier castles where defence was clearly more important than the provision of comfortable accommodation, castles that were dominated by an internal keep, often with several lines or circuits of defences. In contrast, Bodiam's defences are relatively simple and comprise a single, rectangular perimeter wall with the greatest prominence given to the Gatehouse. The corner drum-towers and the intervening rectangular towers clearly enhance the defences, but also serve to fulfil the requirements for well-designed accommodation within the castle. The octagonal turrets surmounting the newel staircase in each tower provided additional height and could have served as look-outs reached by wooden ladders from the heads of stairways.

The River Rother determined the site and orientation of the castle, and water also played an important part in its defences. The wide moat would have precluded attack by mining under the walls, at which the French had become particularly skilled. An attacker could easily have drained the moat, but would still have found its muddy bottom a considerable obstacle to negotiate. The moat, and the other adjacent ponds, possibly part of an original designed landscape surrounding the castle, would also have combined distance from any potential attacker with improved surveillance of the attacker, and would have directed any assault towards the gatehouses and their approaches. Because of this, the approach to the main north Gatehouse, placed on the side furthest from the river, was long and complex, exposing the unshielded right flank of any attacker to both the north and west faces of the castle. Before arriving at the Gatehouse the obstacles of three drawbridges and a strong barbican building with its own portcullis had to be overcome.

The Gatehouse itself bristles with defensive arrangements. Outer gun-ports on the ground floor of each gatehouse tower, and two further small inverted keyhole gun-ports on first and second floors above the gate, and angled to face north-west, cover the rear of the Barbican and the final drawbridge, whilst further gun-ports on either side of the outer portcullis and gate allowed deadly horizontal fire to rake the final few yards before the portcullis is reached. Nor is this all. Any attacker who got this far and attempted to breach the outer portcullis would have been exposed to missiles dropped vertically through the machicolations (holes in the floor of the overhanging parapet) above the gate recess and around the top of the gate towers. The circular gun-ports are very similar to those in the West Gate at Canterbury and Cooling Castle built by Henry Yevele, and it is tempting to see his hand in the design of Bodiam.

Within the Gatehouse passage two further portcullises and two more sets of gates had to be breached before the interior of the castle was penetrated. To achieve this attackers would again

Bodiam Castle from the north-west

Missiles or boiling liquids could be dropped on any attacker through the 'murder holes' in the vaulted ceiling of the Gatehouse

have exposed themselves to missiles or boiling liquids fired or poured through the open *meurtrières* or 'murder holes' in the bosses of the ceiling vaults. The Postern Tower (or rear gatehouse) was similarly defended with a portcullis at the outer end of the gate passage, two lifting or drawbridges, *meurtrières* in its ceiling (now blocked up) and machicolations covering the outer faces of the tower. There are, however, no gun-ports associated with this tower.

In contrast to the two gatehouses, the defences of the rest of the castle are less developed. The walls are certainly substantial, both thick and high, and there are only a few larger windows facing outwards, but there are no arrow loops anywhere in the castle; the windows, including the plain lancet windows, were built as windows and were glazed. Even the wide merlons (the upper sections of the battlements) along the parapet wall are unpierced by arrow loops, although their upper edges are bevelled, perhaps to deflect arrows. (If this was the intention, it is curious that the feature was not repeated in the intervening crenels.) A sixteenth-century iron mortar was found in the eighteenth century and a number of stone cannonballs weighing up to 150lb

dredged out of the moat in 1919. These discoveries suggest that artillery pieces may have been mounted on the tops of some of the towers. (The original mortar is now in the Rotunda Museum at Woolwich Arsenal in London and a replica can be seen in the North-East Tower.) However, Bodiam was built in the very early days of guns and gunpowder, and it is also possible that the tops of the towers could have been intended to serve as platforms for artillery engines such as the *ballista*, a giant bolt-firing catapult, or the *mangonel* or *trébuchet*, which fired stones or other heavy missiles. Some such machines would have been essential if the castle were to defend the river and its wharves. In addition, the projecting towers and the intervening lengths of curtain wall provided protection for archers.

The lay-out of the curtain wall-walk shows the ingenuity of the castle's designer. It does not form a continuous circuit around the wall tops; no more than two lengths of the wall are accessible from any one tower. This arrangement was apparently designed to isolate various parts of the castle in the event of an attack and to separate the lord's apartments on the south and east side from the garrison's quarters on the west.

In replacing the earlier manor house or houses, Bodiam Castle assumed the role of the main residence of Sir Edward Dalyngrigge as lord of the manor. It was, therefore, intended to be not simply a castle with well-designed defences capable of housing a garrison, but also a sophisticated and comfortable home. The surviving fragments of architectural detail, including the doors and windows facing into the central courtyard, hint at the quality of design and construction employed and at what must have been the very pleasing proportions of the castle's interior.

The dual role of the castle as stronghold and residence can perhaps be best understood by looking at the arrangements of rooms within the castle. The rooms themselves are described in Chapter Six. Here we will consider how they may have worked as apartments or lodgings for the residents. A man of Sir Edward's status would have had to provide accommodation not only for his family, but also for the rest of his (predominantly male) 'household'.

This might well have comprised domestic servants, cooks, a falconer, grooms, smiths and stable-boys, a steward, a chaplain and a treasurer as well as knights and esquires in his service – perhaps as many as 150 in all. In addition, he would have had to provide for the households of visiting lords and, when necessary, for a garrison. The arrangement of accommodation provided distinct and independent sets of rooms with their own separate access. Clearly, they would not all have been occupied continuously.

The principal ranges of rooms were laid out within the perimeter wall around a central quadrangle on to which they debouched at ground-floor level, somewhat in the manner of a traditional Oxford or Cambridge college.

The most important room of the castle was the Great Hall, in which the lord would have formally entertained guests and held court. The lord's table was on a raised dais next to the large window at the south-east end of the room, through which the last of the evening sun would have fallen on Sir Edward and his guests at dinner, and from which views over the moat and the lower ponds could be enjoyed.

Replica of the sixteenth-century mortar discovered at Bodiam in the eighteenth century

The Great Hall, of fine proportions, was open to its roof of an elaborate timber construction, perhaps like those which survive in the late thirteenth-century Great Chamber at Old Soar Manor, Kent, or in the impressive mid-fourteenth-century Great Hall at Penshurst Place, also in Kent. The fireplace was perhaps in the courtyard wall opposite this window, or, in this most formal of rooms, may still have comprised a central brazier, the smoke from which would have escaped through a louvred opening in the roof. Other tables for those of lower rank would have been ranged around the walls below the high table. The walls would probably have been plastered and limewashed, and decorated with paintings, perhaps simply representing the coursing of the masonry or with floral patterns or richly coloured historical, chivalric, heraldic or biblical scenes, or by painted woven cloth hangings or tapestries. At the west end was a wooden screen, probably also painted, with the screens passage beyond it, through which most diners would have entered the Great Hall, and a minstrel gallery above.

Sir Edward and his guests may have entered the Great Hall at its east end from a small ante-room at ground-floor level. There are also three related chambers in the South-East Tower, each with a fireplace and a garderobe (a small closet, usually containing a latrine), serving as bedrooms either for the lord's family or for eminent visitors. These may have had access to the ante room adjacent to the hall or living-room that occupied most of the ground floor of the East Range. Beyond the Great Hall a

The Great Hall. Sir Edward Dalyngrigge and his guests would have dined on a raised dais at the east (left-hand) end of the Hall, next to the large window in the exterior wall

The roof of the Great Hall at Bodiam may have resembled that which still survives at Penshurst Place in Kent. Joseph Nash offers a romantic view of medieval life in the Penshurst hall in his 'Mansions of England in the olden time' (1841)

further comfortable chamber, bedroom or office connected directly with the Chapel, and had another bedroom off it on the ground floor of the East Tower. The other principal room on the ground floor of the East Range was the Chapel, lit by a large lancet window facing east, as liturgy demanded. The great cellars below the East Range may have been occupied by household servants, and also been used for storage.

The apartments on the first floor of the East Range seem likely to have been those intended for the personal use of Sir Edward and subsequent lords of the manor, and were probably the most elaborately decorated in the castle. They comprised an ante-chamber at the south end of the range leading on to a hall, the Lord's personal living-room with its elaborate fireplace and large, two-light window. At the north end of the hall was a further chamber with a private pew leading off it and overlooking the Chapel. Two further comfortable bedrooms or chambers in the East Tower, both with fireplaces and garderobes, also belonged to this group of rooms. Little evidence has survived of how such family rooms were furnished. As a soldier Dalyngrigge would have been used to the minimum of folding furniture, and it is doubtful whether the

beds and chairs would have been much more elaborate than those he used on campaign. Tapestries may have hung on the walls. Rush matting would have covered the floor.

Both the Great Hall and the two principal suites of apartments in the East Range were served by the main Kitchen, which, with its Buttery and Pantry, lay behind oak doors beyond the screens passage at the west end of the Great Hall. Ales and wines were dispensed from the Buttery, whilst other necessities of the kitchen were stored in the Pantry. Conveniently placed in the adjacent South-West Tower were the well and the dovecote, the latter yet another indication of the owner's status.

In the east part of the North Range were two further halls on the ground and first floors. Both halls had access to a staircase serving three individual chambers, each with its own fireplace and garderobe, in the North-East Tower. These comfortable apartments were probably for the use of visiting lords and their households; the arrangement perhaps implies that the upper hall and the bedrooms in the North-East Tower were for the visiting lord and the most senior of his retinue, whilst the lower hall, with access to the portcullis chamber in the Gatehouse, was used communally by others of the visiting household, who may have been expected to share, to some extent at least, in the castle's defence.

In addition to the Great Hall and the four other halls described above, there were at least two other substantial halls in the West Range. Between the principal Kitchen and what may have been the Retainers' Kitchen was a ground-floor hall with a long chamber above. These two rooms, which borrowed heat from the two adjacent kitchens, were clearly not of the same status as those in the East or the North Ranges, and may well have been servants' apartments. However, three comfortable, individual chambers in the West Tower led off the ground-floor hall and must have provided good accommodation for perhaps some of the more senior of the domestic staff or of the garrison.

The lay-out of the accommodation in the north-west angle of the castle is now a matter of conjecture. The ground-floor rooms to the north of the 'Retainers' Kitchen' all appear to have been service rooms, perhaps for the garrison, rather than accommodation, although access to the three individual chambers in the North-West Tower was

from the ground floor. A long hall with a fireplace and a garderobe in the north-west angle on the first floor may well have provided eating and sleeping accommodation for a garrison. The single adjacent chamber next to the Gatehouse perhaps housed an officer of the garrison. The room below this on the ground floor has often been claimed to be the stables. The presence of stabling within the castle would have been essential if a garrison was to have any serious military intent. It would also have served visiting lords and their retinues. However, there is not a great deal of room for stabling here, and no trace of drains or stalls, normally associated with stables, was found when the floor was excavated by Curzon.

Within the Gatehouse, at first- and second-floor levels, were two further suites of three rooms. The central chamber on the first floor contained the portcullis winding apparatus, and, since it has a fireplace, perhaps doubled as a communal living-room.

Two further single chambers were available within the Postern Tower; here again, the lower chamber contained the portcullis winding gear.

Although these residential arrangements are complicated and conjectural, it is clear that Bodiam Castle was capable of accommodating a substantial number of people – the lord's own family and household, the retinue of at least one visiting lord, and perhaps up to three at any one time, as well as a sizeable garrison. That the castle was well used can be seen from the wear on the treads of the stone staircases, even those that have not been accessible to visitors for many years, and in the degree of burning in all the firebacks of the many fireplaces. It is perhaps not easy to imagine the castle furnished and full of life, bustle, noise, smells and activity, yet this is how it was for perhaps more than two hundred years after it was built, until the seventeenth century, when it seems it was finally abandoned.

The three arches of the screens passage connected the Great Hall with the Kitchen, Buttery and Pantry

CHAPTER FOUR
THE DECLINE AND RESCUE OF BODIAM

Sir John Dalyngrigge, sometimes described as the 'King's Knight', enjoyed, like his father, Sir Edward, some considerable favour at court. He acted as a royal ambassador, travelling abroad in the service of Henry IV, and represented Sussex in four parliaments. (The family quarrel with Henry's father, John of Gaunt, had clearly been settled by this time.) Sir John received a royal grant in 1400 of 100 marks yearly for life, which was exchanged in 1405 for the custody of the castle and lordship of Bramber in Sussex.

Sir John died on 27 September 1408, leaving a widow, Alice, who had previously been married to Sir Thomas Botiler, and who lived on until 1443. In his will Sir John desired to be buried in the church of the Blessed Mary in the Abbey of Robertsbridge beside the tomb of his father and mother. When the will was finally settled in 1421, a considerable sum was left to Robertsbridge Abbey to be used for the good of Sir John's soul, including the celebration of commemorative masses and the saying of daily prayers. A mutilated alabaster effigy in the castle museum was rediscovered at Robertsbridge in 1823, having been broken up and buried after the dissolution of the Abbey in 1536; it is of the torso of Sir John wearing a surcoat with a 'cross engrailed' upon it, part of the Dalyngrigge coat of arms. Around the neck is a collar with the letters SS upon it, a Lancastrian device that proclaimed his loyalty to Henry IV, the first king of the House of Lancaster.

Sir John's will contained a number of small bequests including one for the repair of the bridge at Bodiam and the adjacent roads. His estates, including Bodiam Castle, were left to his widow Alice for life and, as they had no children, thereafter to his cousin, Richard Dalyngrigge.

During Alice's widowhood, in 1440, there is an interesting reference to the park at Bodiam. A pardon was granted to Richard Brigges of Rolvynden, Kent, for not appearing before the Justices in answer to a plea that he had broken into Alice's park at Bodiam, and hunted there for deer without permission. There are very few references to a deer park at Bodiam; the earliest is in the twelfth century, when the manor was owned by the de Bodeham family. The presence of an associated deer park is yet another expression of Sir Edward Dalyngrigge's status and fits well with the image of Bodiam as a manorial seat of some luxury. There is no trace of the deer park today, although the name survives in South Park and Park Farm in the parish. Presumably it was originally detached from the castle to the west of the village where Park Farm is now situated.

Richard Dalyngrigge inherited the estates on the death of Alice. He was predeceased by his brother William and himself died in 1470. Both brothers died without issue and in accordance with Sir John Dalyngrigge's will the estates therefore passed to their sister Philippa, whose second husband, Sir Thomas Lewknor, of a leading Sussex family, owned property in many parts of the county. There is, unfortunately, very little evidence to suggest whether the successive generations of the Lewknor family who owned Bodiam Castle actually lived there, or, if they did, for what periods. Philippa and Sir Thomas's son, Sir Roger Lewknor, who is recorded as owning the castle in 1473 and who died in 1478, is described as of Dedisham in Slinfold, Sussex.

Sir Roger's eldest son, Sir Thomas Lewknor of Trotton, where there is a memorial to him in the church, came into the ownership of the castle and for a time certainly occupied it. The Wars of the Roses, which had begun in 1455, had divided the country into factions. Sir Thomas chose to support the Lancastrian party, despite the fact that his two

FAMILY TREE OF THE DALYNGRIGGES
AND LEWKNORS

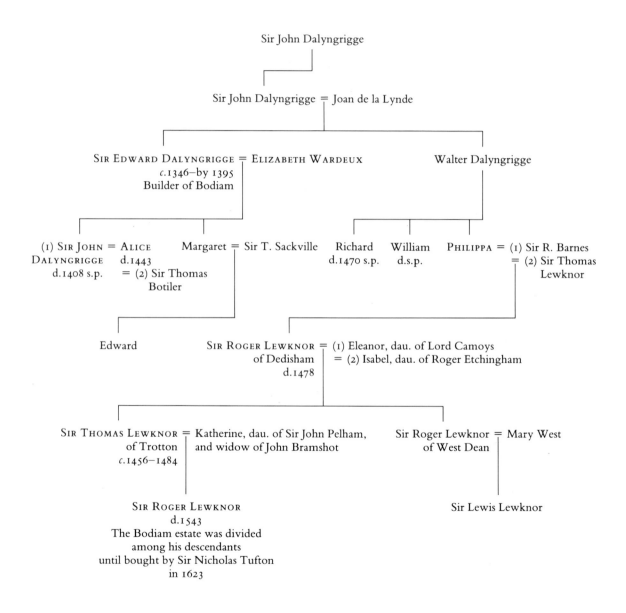

Owners of Bodiam are set in CAPITALS

uncles, another Sir Thomas and Sir Richard Lewk-nor, supported the Yorkist cause of Edward IV and his brother, the Duke of Gloucester. Following the accession to the throne of Gloucester as Richard III in 1483 Sir Thomas was attainted for treason. He was accused of assembling men-at-arms and making 'traitorous proclamations' at Maidstone, Rochester and Guildford in October of that year, in support of the uprising of the rebels of Kent and Surrey against the king. The following month a commission was issued to Thomas Howard, Earl of Surrey (whose family lived at nearby Arundel Castle), and others, including Richard Lewknor of Brambletye, Sir

The tomb brass of Sir Walter and Lady Dalyngrigge (c.1390) in Fletching church, Sussex. Their son, Richard, inherited Bodiam from Sir John Dalyngrigge

The mutilated remains of the tomb effigy of Sir John Dalyngrigge, who was buried at Robertsbridge Abbey, 3 miles south-west of Bodiam

Thomas's uncle, 'to levy men in the Counties of Kent and Sussex to besiege the Castle of Bodiam which the rebels have seized'.

There is no record that the castle was besieged and it seems likely that Sir Thomas surrendered without putting up much, if any, resistance. By August 1484 Nicholas Rigby, one of the Yeomen of the Crown, was appointed constable of the castle, a post for which he appears to have been drawing a salary since the previous December. The appointment was for life with a salary of £20 per annum and with all profits derived from the park at Bodiam. It has been argued that following this episode the castle was dismantled, but when Lord Curzon carried out his excavation of the castle and the moat he found evidence that occupation had continued into the seventeenth century.

Nicholas Rigby's constableship was short-lived. It must have been revoked in 1485 following Richard III's defeat at the Battle of Bosworth. The new King, Henry VII, the first of the Tudor monarchs, quickly reversed the attainder of Sir Thomas, who was reinstated, but it was not until 1542, more than half a century later, that his son Sir Roger, who had become Sheriff of Sussex in 1532, regained the full possession of the lordship of Bodiam. Sir Roger died a month later, and the manor and castle were split into two, and sometimes more, moieties, or separate ownerships, by the frequent marriages and deaths of the Lewknor family. Curzon has traced the complicated descent of title of the various ownerships of the parts of the manor and castle throughout the sixteenth and seventeenth centuries, but unfortunately his researches throw no light on how the castle itself was used.

In 1623 Sir Nicholas Tufton, who later became the 1st Earl of Thanet, acquired by purchase the majority share of the estate. He was succeeded in 1631 by his son John, who reunited the castle and manor in 1639 for the first time in a hundred years. Sir John Tufton, 2nd Earl of Thanet and an ardent Royalist, commanded an attack against Lewes in December 1642, and was seriously defeated at Haywards Heath. In 1643 and 1644 various of his possessions were seized by Parliament, including estates and woodland and his houses at Windsor, Heathfield and London, and in October 1644 he was fined £9,000. Presumably in order to pay this fine, he sold the castle of Bodiam with its appurtenances, together with the manor, to Nathaniel Powell for £6,000 in March 1644.

The dismantling of Bodiam Castle must have occurred around this time, although there is, sadly, no evidence for it, even in the records of the County Committee which may have issued the instructions. Curzon put forward a strong argument that it took place during the ownership of Nathaniel Powell, who was a Parliamentarian and Gunfounder to the State, and may have purchased the estate for its land. Certainly, there is no evidence that he ever intended to live in the castle.

There are numerous examples of castles, residences and defences deliberately dismantled during and after the Civil War to make them undefend-

The ruins of the Chapel; watercolour by S. H. Grimm, 1784 (British Museum). Following the dismantling of the fortifications during the Civil War, Bodiam declined into a picturesque ivy-clad ruin

The Barbican and north front; watercolour by S. H. Grimm, 1784 (British Museum)

able, the majority ordered by Parliament. However, there are cases where work carried out was slight or where, as at Bolsover in Derbyshire, the castle was ordered to be made untenable without unnecessary spoiling or defacing. At Bodiam it is possible that the dismantling of the bridges and the interior buildings, and perhaps the partial demolition of the Barbican, were considered sufficient to make the castle untenable. The bridges had certainly gone by the mid-eighteenth century, when the castle was first portrayed by topographical draughtsmen, who show it as an ivy-clad ruin, lacking battlements, and with a causeway to the Barbican following the line of the present access bridge, and not that of the original. Apart from the moat, the other waterscape features around the castle appear to have been drained by this time.

Despite his Parliamentary sympathies, Nathaniel Powell was made a Baronet by Charles II in 1661, soon after the Restoration, and died in 1674–5. Bodiam passed to his son Sir Nathaniel Powell, 2nd Baronet, and then to the 2nd Baronet's daughter-in-law, Elizabeth Clitherow and her younger son Christopher, who held the estate until it was sold again soon after 1722 to Sir Thomas Webster of Battle Abbey in Sussex.

The Webster family owned castle and manor for over a hundred years. It was during the period of their ownership that Bodiam began to attract increasing interest from those who saw it as a picturesque reminder of England's medieval glories. The intrepid traveller Lord Torrington paid a visit in 1788. On 'a dark day with a howling wind unpleasant for tourists' he came to see 'the noble remains of the square castle of Bodiham', but had a frustrating time:

This castle belongs to Sr Godfrey Webster, who has lock'd up the gate leading into the interior of the

The interior looking east; watercolour by S. H. Grimm, 1784 (British Museum)

square; and from a narrowness of possession does not allow a key to any neighbour; tho, surely a proper inhabitant wou'd secure, and preserve it, and get a livelyhood, (or at least much support,) from us, castle hunters. So I cou'd only walk around the little lake which washes the building; and adds much to the curiosity, and safety of the building.

Architects and their patrons were also turning back to the great Plantagenet castles like Bodiam as the source of inspiration for the renovation of historic palaces such as Windsor or the creation of new country houses. The engravings of the Buck brothers and the drawings and watercolours of S. H. Grimm and James Lambert are vivid witness to this new enthusiasm, but they also provide a very useful impression of the state of the ivy-clad castle ruins in the late eighteenth century. The Burrell

MSS in the British Museum refer to the building of a cottage against the Postern Tower within the castle. A drawing by Lambert of 1782 shows the cottage in question, with smoke spiralling from its chimney and with much of the central courtyard planted with neat rows of vegetables and borders of fruit trees tended by a gardener and his wife, who both seem to feature in the watercolours of Grimm two years later.

The third Sir Godfrey Webster attempted to sell the property in 1815 and finally achieved the sale of the castle and 24 acres of adjoining land in 1829 to John Fuller of Rosehill in the parish of Brightling, Sussex, for £3,000. (Fuller's copy of the auction particulars was recently given to the Trust by a descendant.) Fuller is thought to have bought the castle to save it from being dismantled by the Websters and the stone used for building. He is recorded as having provided new folding oak gates in the front doorway of the Gatehouse, and also as having restored the Postern Tower, presumably by removing the cottage which was there 50 years earlier. These were the first positive moves to protect the ruins, an intention that was pursued more vigorously by George Cubitt, who purchased the castle and 24 acres from John Fuller's grandson for something over £5,000 in 1864. The Cubitt family already had an interest in the area; George Cubitt's father, Thomas, had purchased the church living in 1849 for the Rev. C. Parker, who had married his daughter, Mary, in 1846. George Cubitt, created Lord Ashcombe in 1892, continued to buy land in the locality until 1907, and undertook a considerable amount of work on the castle.

Lord Curzon, who bought Bodiam Castle in 1916 and bequeathed it to the National Trust

Having commissioned a detailed survey of the castle by J. Tavernor Perry in 1864, Cubitt undertook the repair of much of the exterior of the castle, which was in very poor condition. He drained the moat and discovered many of the stones of the parapet, which he reinstated, also replacing, with new Wadhurst stone, missing ashlar facing blocks of the curtain wall. He employed a mason, Charles Thompson, who was also the local schoolmaster and worked under the direction of Cubitt's brother-in-law, Mr Parker. The interior of the south-west corner tower had almost completely collapsed, and in places the external walls themselves survived only a single stone in thickness. Cubitt restored the dovecote at the top of the South-West Tower, but did not attempt to dig out the rubble at the base of the tower, where he would have found the well. This discovery was left to Curzon. The repairs to the mullions of the three-light pointed east window in the Chapel were undertaken as well as those to the Buttery windows facing into the courtyard. The Postern Tower was repaired and made safe and accessible to visitors. But the fashion for ivy clad ruins still remained and Cubitt resisted the total clearance of ivy and of trees growing in the courtyard, to the detriment of the masonry. Harold Sands, writing in 1903, refers to a visit to the castle by the Sussex Archaeological Society, and appeals almost passionately:

It is to be wished that his Lordship *would* give orders for the removal of the ivy which conceals the interior walls, and will, if not checked, level them with the ground, seeing that so much has been done by him in the way of careful repair, and restoration in the Wadhurst stone, of which the castle is built, since his purchase of the property in 1864.

Lord Curzon was enchanted by Bodiam from the moment he first saw it, possibly during his brief period of Wardenship of the Cinque Ports in 1905, following his return from serving as Viceroy of India. He determined that 'so rare a treasure should neither be lost to our country nor desecrated by irreverent hands', and made enquiries of Lord Ashcombe to see if the castle could be purchased. Lord Ashcombe had no intention of selling it during his lifetime, but after his death Lord Curzon was

The Barbican as it appeared when Curzon first came to Bodiam

Lord Curzon drained the moat to reveal the footings of the original bridge connecting the western abutment to the Octagon

able to negotiate with his son, and finally acquired Bodiam Castle and the surrounding lands in 1916.

In her autobiography, *Reminiscences*, Grace Curzon tells of her first visit to Bodiam with Curzon in a passage which describes better than any his feelings for the castle, and indeed those of his wife to be, for that afternoon following the visit to Bodiam he proposed marriage in the beautiful setting of Winchelsea Church:

One day in the summer of 1916, just before I was leaving 32 Grosvenor Square to move to Trent Park, George asked me to motor with him to see Bodiam Castle. As we approached the hill leading down to Bodiam village, the chauffeur was told to drive very slowly while George looked for an opening he remembered between the trees by the roadside.

Suddenly he told the chauffeur to stop and we got out; and turning to me he said, 'Now give me your hand, and climb up this bank, with your eyes closed, and don't open them until I tell you.' He helped me up the bank, and then said 'Now, look!' I have that picture in my heart for all time. Looking down on the castle was like looking into another world, I can find no words to describe the beauty. It was a heavenly summer morning, and I felt, as I looked at this divinely inspired picture, that I dared not take my eyes off it, for fear that when I looked again it would have disappeared in a mist or a cloud – it could only be a fairy castle.

We drove into the grounds, and spent an hour or more while George, more excited than I had ever seen him before, described all that he hoped to do to restore Bodiam to its original magnificence, so that its beauty might last for ever.

Lord Curzon embarked on the work of research and restoration with his architect William Weir in 1919. Weir had already worked with him on a considerable restoration programme at Tattershall

29

Castle, Lincolnshire, which Curzon had acquired in 1911 and which he also bequeathed to the National Trust. In June work began with the draining of the moat and excavation of the thick layer of mud at the bottom in order to examine the castle's foundations. This exercise was carried out with great care so as to save the considerable number of fish in the moat, including pike weighing as much as 15lb, and 'eels of a great age' (but to Curzon's great surprise no carp). The depth of water was 5 feet on average, up to 7 feet near the south-east corner, with upwards of 3 feet of mud above the bed of the moat. The moat is fed by springs, which rise to the north-west of the castle and enter the moat just south of the bridge abutment opposite the Octagon, and by others rising from the bed of the moat itself. These caused some problems for the workmen, whose job was made even more difficult by the extensive mats of foul-smelling water-lily roots. None the less, the task was achieved and Curzon's workmen discovered the footings of the two original bridges, that from the western abutment to the Octagon and the southern bridge to the Postern Tower. He was able to make careful drawings of these and to recover a number of coping stones which indicated that both the western abutment and the Octagon had parapets, as well as some of those missing from the battlements of the castle itself. The bases of the castle walls were carefully repointed and the banks of the moat were repaired and reinforced.

Amongst the finds Curzon made from the moat was an enormous stone shot, 14 inches in diameter (see page 16) and other stone and iron cannonballs, iron tools and fragments of pottery, which Curzon took as evidence of the castle's occupation into the seventeenth century. Many of these are now on display in the castle museum.

Within the castle Curzon's workmen dug out the basement of the South-West Tower to discover the well, the masonry of which was repaired. Excavations were carried out in the Chapel to reveal the arrangement of the sanctuary, nave and crypt, in the basements of the North-East Range, the East Range, the Buttery, the West Tower and the West Range, the North-West Tower and the twin Gatehouse towers. Ground levels were established, the ground levelled and turfed, and quantities of ivy, bushes and some trees were removed. A single hawthorn tree on the east side was allowed to remain as 'it was found to be doing no damage to the fabric and added a touch of pleasant greenery to the scene'. The tree finally collapsed in 1952. Considerable repairs were also carried out to the stonework, where required, using stone quarried near West Hoathley in Sussex.

Outside the castle, beyond the moat, Curzon excavated the sunken area to the south-east of the castle close to the River Rother, which is referred to as the old 'Harbour', using the soil excavated from its base to form a dam across its southern end. He built a sluice into this new bank, levelled the tops of the original banks to form footpaths and had the 'Harbour' flooded.

In the adjacent large sunken area to the west, which was probably the mill-pond and which he referred to as the 'Tiltyard', Curzon attempted, unsuccessfully, to provide drainage in order to turn it into a cricket ground. (These earthwork features beyond the moat are described in Chapter Seven.)

Curzon also carried out works on the setting of the castle, having retained the ownership of the surrounding fields, particularly those on the west between the castle and the village. Here fences and hedges were removed and trees planted to create the park-like setting which we see today. Having achieved this immense task of repair, Curzon built the castle cottage to house a custodian and created a small museum in part of it to house the collection of objects from the excavations, and of drawings, photographs and engravings which he had collected. These form the nucleus of the present museum.

Since 1925 the Trust has continued the work of restoring Bodiam put in hand by Lord Curzon. New roofs were added to the East Tower in 1932–3, and to the North-West Tower in 1936, and the Gatehouse was reroofed in 1939. The moat was once again drained in 1970, and further excavation carried out by David Martin and the Robertsbridge and District Archaeological Society. Floors have also been reintroduced to parts of the Gatehouse to give the visitor a better idea of how the interior of the castle appeared in medieval times.

CHAPTER FIVE
THE HERALDRY

Bodiam Castle's combination of military strength and sophisticated domestic architecture proclaimed the status of its builder, Sir Edward Dalyngrigge. To emphasise that status, Sir Edward incorporated shields of arms on the outside of both the Gatehouse and the Postern Tower as an expression of the antiquity of his own and his wife's noble descent and of his loyalty to Sir Robert Knollys, his former campaigning captain.

Above the outer gate of the Gatehouse are carved in relief three coats of arms. These may have been coloured originally.

The central shield bears the arms of Sir Edward Dalyngrigge, described in heraldic terms as: *or*, on a cross engrailed *gules*, a cross billetty (on a gold field, a red cross with concave scalloped edges, with a superimposed cross of billets or bars). Above this is a tilting or tournament helmet with Sir Edward's crest, a unicorn's head. The inclusion of a helmet denoted that Sir Edward had the necessary resources to participate in tournaments and is a further

Wardeux   *Dalyngrigge*   *Radynden*

Knollys

expression of his pedigree and aristocratic status. The unicorn, always considered a sacred symbol of purity and virtue, the symbol of Christ, was little used until the end of the fourteenth century because of these associations, but became more common thereafter. Sir Edward may have employed it as a further expression of his strength, through self-acclaimed virtue, against his foes.

To the left of the Dalyngrigge arms is the shield of arms of the Wardeux or Wardedieu family. Through his marriage to Elizabeth Wardeux, Sir Edward acquired the manor and lordship of Bodiam. This is described as: *argent* a fesse dancetty *sable*, bezanty (on a silver field, a zig-zag black band with a pattern of gold roundels).

To the right of Sir Edward's arms are the arms of Radynden. Sir Edward inherited the Manor of Radynden from Sir Roger Dalyngrigge, who was probably a cousin and who was Sheriff of Sussex in 1333. Sir Roger obtained the Radynden Manor through his marriage to Alice, daughter and heir of Sir John de Radynden, some time before 1350. This is described as: *sable* six martlets *or* three, two, one (on a black field, six gold heraldic birds depicted without feet representing the swallow or martin, which it was believed never landed on the ground. These are arranged in descending rows of three, two, one.)

On the Postern Tower are three more shields carved in relief. The outer two are both blank; the centre one tilted sideways is the coat of arms of Sir Robert Knollys, under whom Sir Edward Dalyngrigge served in France. Its presence at Bodiam is a mark of allegiance to his former leader. His arms are described as: *gules*, a chevron *argent*, three roses *gules* (a red field with a silver chevron across it bearing three red roses), and they are surmounted by a mantled tilting or tournament helm with a ram's head crest.

PLAN OF THE CASTLE

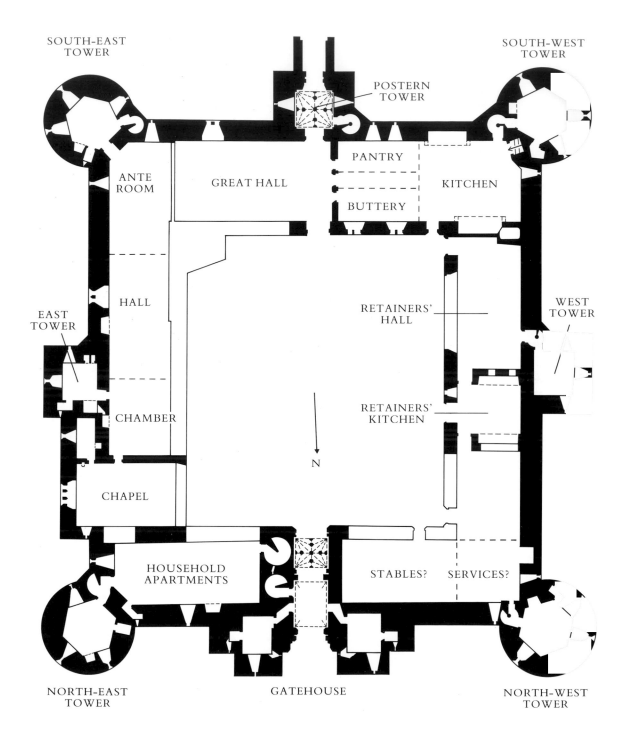

SOUTH-EAST TOWER

SOUTH-WEST TOWER

POSTERN TOWER

ANTE ROOM

GREAT HALL

PANTRY

KITCHEN

BUTTERY

HALL

RETAINERS' HALL

WEST TOWER

EAST TOWER

CHAMBER

RETAINERS' KITCHEN

N

CHAPEL

HOUSEHOLD APARTMENTS

STABLES?

SERVICES?

NORTH-EAST TOWER

GATEHOUSE

NORTH-WEST TOWER

CHAPTER SIX

THE CASTLE

The first impression of Bodiam is one of great strength and symmetry. A compact building, it is defended by a broad, water-filled moat, and, reflected in it, a defensive arrangement of towers linked by curtain wall. At the corners are circular drum-towers which derive much of their strength of form from their proportions; each occupies a fifth of the length of each side. Rectangular towers are placed centrally. On the south side the central tower houses the Postern Gate, originally connected by a timber bridge and drawbridge to the south bank of the moat.

On the north side this impression is increased by the magnificent twin rectangular towers of the Gatehouse, which dominates access into the castle.

Again the sense of symmetry is impressive; the twin towers of the Gatehouse occupy over a third of the length of the wall, with the intervening sections of curtain wall no more than short links between the Gatehouse and corner towers.

The Approach

The Gatehouse is approached today across the moat by a timber bridge from the north bank to an octagonal island outwork, the Octagon. From there a further bridge connects with the Barbican, another island in the moat, on which there are traces of a vaulted gateway. A second timber bridge provides the final link to the Gatehouse.

Bodiam Castle from the south-west. The central Postern Tower was originally connected by a bridge to the south bank of the moat

The foundations of the original bridge excavated by Curzon

THE BRIDGES

The present bridges are modern; the shorter gaps must originally have been spanned by drawbridges. The long bridge from the north bank to the Octagon replaces a causeway which was not original, but had been built by 1750, as it is shown in the Buck engraving of that date. The medieval access was at right angles to the present line on a timber bridge from an abutment on the west bank. This was a long ceremonial approach, built in the military fashion to expose the unshielded right flank of any attacker to the castle's defenders standing along the parapets of the north and west walls. It would also have provided a fitting climax to the arrival of more friendly visitors whose approach from the river may have been along the causeways and banks between areas of water now visible only as the dry outlines of ponds, designed to enhance the castle's setting and dramatic impact.

The original bridge arrangements were first discovered by Lord Curzon, when he emptied the moat in 1919–20 and revealed the foundations for the wooden trestles which carried the bridges. Those to the Postern Gate from the south bank of the moat were of dry-stone construction, whilst the bridge from the stone-faced abutment on the west bank across to the Octagon was built on timber sill-beams.

The main entrance bridge, 136 feet long, was of fixed construction for ten of its eleven spans, the final span being covered by a drawbridge across to the masonry abutment on the west bank. The oak beams which supported the trestles carrying the bridge were very well preserved in the moat silt. They had been placed in trenches dug at right angles to the line of the bridge about 11 feet apart. Those supporting the continuous trestle bridge typically had two pairs of mortice holes to take two upright beams, with a supporting outer strut. The westernmost sill-beam was of a more complex construction, designed to carry the frame and winding gear for a drawbridge. The bridge itself was carefully dismantled, leaving only the sill-beams in the mud.

Further excavations were carried out by David Martin and the Robertsbridge and District Archaeological Society when the moat was again drained in 1970. These excavations confirmed most of Lord Curzon's findings and from them a detailed reconstruction of the drawbridge was drawn. They also demonstrated that the original bridges were built in two phases. The first consisted of a continuous timber bridge from the Octagon to the west bank, without the abutment and the drawbridge. This presumably provided site access for the castle builders. The west end of the bridge was then taken down, the abutment built against the bank and the drawbridge constructed shortly after as work on the castle defences was finalised. These two phases are also seen in the building of the Barbican and causeway across to the Gatehouse.

THE OCTAGON

It was not clear from the excavations what defences would have been provided for the Octagon, although both excavations found coping-stones for a parapet. The footings for a garderobe (or latrine) chute were discovered on the north-east side, implying that a guard would have been posted here when necessary. The Octagon would have provided room for turning a wagon and team. From the Octagon a further short bridge, probably a drawbridge, connected with the Barbican. There is no clear trace today of how this bridge worked.

THE BARBICAN

This was built as a two-storey gatehouse to give additional protection to the Gatehouse itself. Only the lower part of the west wall survives. This does, however, include the jamb stones framing the arches at either end of the passage which, strangely, contain no sign of hinge fittings for gates in the stonework. There is also the slot for a portcullis outside the north door and traces of a circular newel staircase in the north-west corner. The base of a garderobe chute on the east side hints at some degree of comfort for the guard chamber on the first floor. Drawings by S. H. Grimm in 1784 show the lower storey surviving, complete with details of the vaulting in the passageway.

David Martin's excavations showed that the

S. H. Grimm's 1784 watercolour shows the vaulting of the Barbican still intact (British Museum)

causeway, between the Barbican and the Gatehouse, was built to replace a timber bridge soon after the initial building. Masons' marks on the stonework of the causeway indicate that the same masons were involved in both phases of work. A third timber bridge, again presumably a drawbridge, provided the final link to the Gatehouse, although, again, the evidence for how it would have worked is tantalisingly lacking.

As with the main entrance, the gate in the Postern Tower was connected to a stone-faced abutment on the south bank by a fixed bridge of seven bays with a further bay covered by a drawbridge. In this case, the wooden trestles were supported on dry-stone plinths rather than dug into the bottom of the moat. The arrangement of the foundations for the drawbridge structure closely resembles in plan that of the main entrance drawbridge.

THE GATEHOUSE

No one could doubt that the Gatehouse was designed to imply defensive strength. The approach, as we have seen, demanded the negotiation of two drawbridges and a long, exposed bridge, the defensive Barbican building with its own portcullis and two gates, and finally a further drawbridge exposed to machicolations above and gun-loops in the walls flanking the doorway itself. Yet for all its forbidding strength it has a quality of design which makes it an aesthetic and an architectural masterpiece.

EXTERIOR

The Gatehouse is on three levels, with further basement rooms below the main guard chambers. The central entrance passage is flanked by project-

ing rectangular towers protected from above by a machicolated and crenellated parapet carried on corbels. The machicolations are carried across the outer wall of the entrance passage, above the gate, by a high, chamfered arch. Within the recess formed by this arch are two simple, double-chamfered lancet windows on first and second floors with, between them, a fine relief carving of a tilting helm surmounted by a unicorn's head, Sir Edward Dalyngrigge's crest. Beneath the lower window are three coats of arms carved in relief; the arms of Dalyngrigge in the centre, with those of Wardeux on the left and Radynden on the right. (The heraldry of these is discussed in Chapter Five.)

Beneath the shields and framing the doorway is a further rectangular recess with chamfered edges. It has been argued in the past that this was designed

The approach to the Gatehouse

originally to house the lifted drawbridge, but the space is hardly large enough, and we must assume that it was never used for this purpose. Certainly no mechanisms for lifting a drawbridge were incorporated into the masonry around the doorway.

Within the recess a tall four-centred arch with chamfered inner edge screens the medieval, outer portcullis made of iron-clad oak. A second similar but lower archway for the outer gates lies immediately behind the portcullis. The outer gates, the first of three that originally closed the entrance passage, were replaced by John Fuller in the 1820s.

THE ENTRANCE PASSAGE

This is of two bays, both originally with stone groined and ribbed vaults. The vaulting of the outer bay is incomplete, but that of the inner bay survives intact. The central boss and the bosses at the intersection of the intermediate ribs are pierced with circular holes and those in the ribs against the walls with half-round holes. A similar arrangement existed in the outer bay. These holes are known as *meurtrières* or 'murder holes', through which missiles, caustic slaked lime or boiling liquids such as tar or water, could be poured on any attacker who had penetrated the outer defences.

Between the two bays was provision for a second portcullis behind a second, outer gateway, whilst at the end of the second bay the pattern is repeated, with a third gateway and portcullis so the Gatehouse could be isolated and held against attack from the inside in the event of treachery or an attacking force penetrating the Postern Gate or scaling the walls; altogether a formidable defensive arrangement.

GROUND-FLOOR ROOMS

In the outer bay of the passage are doors into the two high-ceilinged guard chambers on either side. These rooms both have joist holes about two-thirds of the way up the walls. The function of these is unclear, but they may have supported a lower ceiling with storage space above. Both guard chambers have the same arrangement of gun-loops. Those facing north across the moat and commanding the bridge and Barbican are of simple, inverted, key-hole pattern with a short slit for sighting and a circular hole

One of the gun-loops in the Gatehouse

(*oillet*) at the bottom. The gun-loops flanking the doorway have circular holes at both top and bottom. They are set at the end of embrasures in the walls with splayed sides and a flat bottom on which the guns could have been mounted. In addition, both guard chambers have a garderobe leading off them, and these too are provided with small gun-loops.

During his excavations Lord Curzon dug out small prison cells 10 feet deep, which had become infilled, in the basements below the guard chambers, each lit only by a single, tiny, slit window. Access to these cells, which are not open to the public, can only have been through trap-doors in the floors of the guard chambers.

A second doorway on the left of the outer bay of the passage leads to a stair-well which gives access to the upper storeys of the Gatehouse.

The North Range, showing the originally two-storey addition to the Gatehouse

FIRST-FLOOR ROOMS

At first-floor level the stair lobby opens on to the portcullis room and has a groined vault with a fine boss carved in the form of a flower. A small gun-loop in an embrasure in the north wall of this small ante-room commands a view north-west over the Barbican and entrance bridge.

Above the outer bay of the gate passage is the portcullis room where the mechanisms for raising and lowering the outer and middle portcullises were housed. This room has single lancet windows at front and rear and a fireplace in the west wall.

Access to the chamber above the eastern guard chamber is also from the lobby. This room has a

single trefoil-headed window within a splayed opening, a fireplace in the west wall and an adjoining garderobe on the east.

Beyond the portcullis room is a further chamber over the western guard chamber. This room has a garderobe, and a single trefoil-headed lancet window in a wide embrasure but no fireplace.

SECOND-FLOOR ROOMS

On the second floor is a further suite of three rooms. The floors were reconstructed in 1977 as nearly as possible in their original form, and these rooms give some idea of what the interior of the castle would have been like when it was inhabited. The main chamber over the portcullis room has a fireplace, a pair of trefoil-headed lancet windows overlooking the courtyard and a single plain lancet looking north over the moat. The second-storey chamber of the east gatehouse tower repeats the pattern of the room below with a fireplace and garderobe, both on the east side, but has a pair of trefoil-headed lancet windows looking into the courtyard and a single plain lancet looking outwards to the north.

The chamber within the west tower has a single cusped lancet window looking inwards, a plain lancet window looking outwards, and an adjoining garderobe. The parapet walk is reached by steps down from this room, the exit protected by a high merlon, or battlement. This length of the parapet walk connects only with the North-West Tower, where again the steps are hidden from the outside by a high merlon.

The staircase in the Gatehouse, as in all the towers, finishes in a turret giving access to the lead roof and in this case the machicolations over the external wall faces.

ADDITION TO THE GATEHOUSE

The second bay of the entrance passage was originally a two-storey structure built against the rear of the Gatehouse as a modification during the course of construction or very soon after the gateway was built. Access to the first-floor chamber, which no longer survives, was by a circular newel staircase from the ground-floor chamber on the east of the passage. The staircase has been blocked by a later buttress repair, possibly nineteenth-century work

carried out by Fuller or Cubitt. The holes for the *meurtrières* are set into the floor of this chamber which would have blocked the interior window of the portcullis room over the outer bay. The horizontal roof-crease for the lead flashing of this addition is visible from the courtyard just above the first-floor window, and some of the original lead is still in place. The staircase also gave access to the first-floor rooms in the North-East Range.

The Interior of the Castle

In contrast with the exterior, the interior of the castle is in ruins. The domestic buildings which ranged around the central courtyard have been largely dismantled, leaving little more than the arrangements of doors, windows and fireplaces on the inside of the curtain wall to suggest the original layout. On the south side, opposite the main entrance, the inner courtyard wall survives with the Great Hall doorway and inner doors and windows of the kitchen range in the south-west corner. Elsewhere, the inner courtyard wall survives only as footings indicating the width of the buildings. Similarly, very few of the cross-walls survive, and the layout of individual rooms on ground- and first-floor levels is a matter of surmise in several parts of the castle.

Despite this, it is clear that rooms were arranged in suites, including halls, living-rooms, and bed-

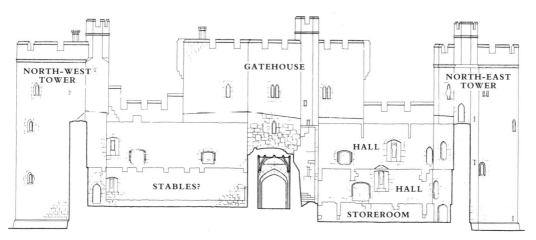

THE NORTH RANGE

The East Range, which contained the Chapel and the apartments of the lord of the manor

chambers, incorporating the towers, and intended for the various groups of people within the castle, including the lord and his family's residence; chambers for important guests and officers of the lord's household; servants' quarters and rooms for a military garrison. (These arrangements are discussed in more detail in Chapter Three.)

The following tour describes the buildings in a clockwise direction from the Gatehouse.

THE NORTH-EAST RANGE (HOUSEHOLD APARTMENTS) AND NORTH-EAST TOWER

To the east of the Gatehouse, the North-East Range has accommodation on two levels, with a basement beneath.

The basement was probably a storeroom. It had access from the courtyard and was lit and ventilated by a pair of tiny windows looking out to the courtyard. It also had a doorway to an hexagonal basement room with two tiny slit windows in the North-East Tower.

The ground-floor chamber ran the full length of the range from the Gatehouse to the North-East Tower. Access was up several steps from the courtyard. This substantial hall contained a fireplace and a single trefoil-headed lancet window in a broad splayed embrasure in its north wall. In the tower angle at the east end is a door leading to a garderobe, and in the east wall a door leading to a newel staircase in the North-East Tower with access to the ground-floor tower chamber. There is also a single lancet window in the east wall. The hexagonal chamber in the North-East Tower, presumably a

(Opposite page) The east window of the Chapel

bedchamber associated with the hall at this level, has a separate garderobe, a fireplace and three single lancet windows in splayed embrasures. These features all suggest that it was quite a comfortable room; indeed all the domestic rooms in the corner towers would have been comfortably furnished.

On the first floor was a similar hall with access from the staircase in the North-East Tower. Both halls were therefore closely linked. Again this hall boasted a fireplace and garderobe, windows in north and east walls and access up a step into the North-East Tower with hexagonal chambers at both first- and second-floor levels, both with fireplaces, garderobes and two single lancet windows. From the second floor there was access to the two adjacent sections of the curtain wall-walk. Both halls would have received additional light from windows looking into the courtyard.

The ground-floor room of the North-East Tower now houses a replica of the early sixteenth-century iron mortar, discovered at Bodiam in the eighteenth century.

THE CHAPEL

Aligned east-west in accordance with liturgical practice, the Chapel was accommodated by a 9-foot projection in the curtain wall which extended as far as the square East Tower. It was divided into two parts, a sanctuary or chancel at the east, raised slightly above the height of the nave and with a solid floor, and a nave with a crypt below it. The sanctuary was originally floored with small glazed tiles, fragments of which can be seen in the museum.

The Chapel has a large pointed east window, partially restored by George Cubitt in the nineteenth century, with three plain pointed lights and a small single-light window in the north wall of the projection over the moat. In the south wall of the sanctuary is an arched piscina. This basin was used by the priest to rinse the communion vessels and has fine, double-chamfered mouldings with chamfer stops. The projecting bowl of the piscina has been cut away, exposing a central drain. At ground-floor level in the south wall of the sanctuary is a plain pointed doorway with a single chamfer moulding,

leading into the Sacristy, a small room used by the priest which was built into the projection of the curtain wall between the Chapel and the East Tower. This room has a plain rectangular cupboard or aumbry in its interior wall and a single-light window looking east over the moat.

Above the Sacristy is a window of two trefoiled lights in a square frame looking into the Chapel from a private pew or oratory, which would have been used by the lord and his family, who occupied the first-floor chambers of the East Range. A door in the south wall of the nave gave direct access to the ground-floor rooms of the East Range.

The crypt has the footings for a partition wall running east to west close to its south side. This defined a narrow passage with a small window looking out into the courtyard and connected to the basement of the East Range by a wide doorway. The reasons for this arrangement are unclear.

THE EAST RANGE (PRINCIPAL APARTMENTS) AND EAST TOWER

The East Range to the south of the Chapel contained the principal living-rooms for Sir Edward Dalyngrigge and subsequent lords of the manor, on two floors with a basement below. The precise layout of these rooms is not at all clear and interpretations have varied. Curzon and others considered that there were two long rooms on each floor; on the ground floor these were referred to as the 'Lady's Bower' adjacent to the Chapel, with the 'Armourie' or 'Great Chamber' to the south. At first-floor level the two rooms have been called the 'Principal Bed Chamber' with the 'Lord's Solar' (or parlour) to the south. More recently it has been suggested that there were possibly three chambers at each level, although Curzon's labels may still be appropriate. The more recent interpretation is used here.

FIRST-FLOOR ROOMS

Access to the first-floor rooms of the East Range was from a circular newel staircase in the south-east angle of the courtyard. This gave direct access from within the Great Hall to a range of rooms that belonged to the lord of Bodiam.

The staircase rose to an ante-room at the south end of the range with two single-light windows in the east wall and one single-light window in the south wall. This room would have been contained in the corner angle of the East and South ranges with the staircase tower in the courtyard against its outer, courtyard wall, and therefore presumably had no windows looking inwards to the courtyard.

North of the ante-room was a further hall, the lord's private hall, with a two-light window incorporating a stone window seat in the east wall adjacent to a grand fireplace, the largest in the castle outside the kitchens. This fireplace was decorated with hollow-chamfered mouldings around its opening. The voussoirs of the fireplace are joggled, or cut for additional decoration, and over it is a projecting crenellated hood.

Beyond this, a further chamber, the Great Chamber, contained a doorway leading to the East Tower, a smaller fireplace and a second doorway giving access to the private pew or oratory overlooking the chancel of the Chapel, above the Sacristy. The Great Chamber had no windows in its east wall because of the position of the East Tower, but both it and the adjacent hall would have had windows overlooking the courtyard.

In the East Tower were two bedchambers at first- and second-floor levels which belonged to this range, both with a garderobe, fireplace and two lancet windows looking east and south. That on the second floor had a doorway with steps down giving access to the north-east curtain wall-walk and to the North-East Tower.

GROUND-FLOOR ROOMS

Access to the ground-floor rooms of the East Range was from a doorway in the south wall of the Chapel.

The northernmost chamber, again lit originally by windows in the courtyard wall, had a fireplace in the east wall and a door giving access to a single, square room on the ground floor of the East Tower. This latter room was a bedchamber and had a garderobe, two small cupboards in the south wall, single lancet windows to east and south, and was heated by a small arched opening from the rear of the fireplace in the room outside.

A hall at ground-floor level, to the south of the East Tower, had a two-light window with a stone window seat adjacent to a fine fireplace. This substantial room must have had further windows facing into the courtyard and a doorway giving direct access out into the courtyard.

Beyond this hall, at the south end of the range, the ground-floor chamber contained single-light windows in the south and east walls, flanking the doorway into the South-East Tower. It is unclear whether there was access from the Great Hall through to this room and to the South-East Tower, or indeed, whether there was necessarily access

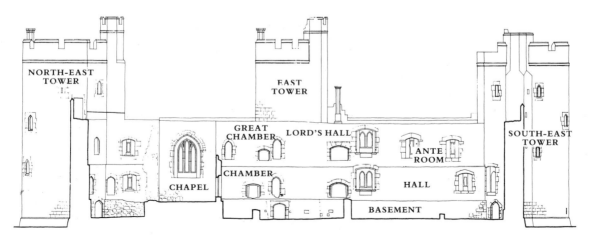

THE EAST RANGE

between this room, the ante-room to the South-East Tower and the hall and suite of rooms to the north.

BASEMENT ROOMS

There were four basement rooms in the East Range, which were probably used for storage; the southernmost was lit by a small window in the south curtain wall and the others by single narrow windows into the courtyard. Access into the basements was down from the Great Hall by the newel staircase in the south-east corner of the courtyard and through two doorways which gave direct access from the courtyard, either by ramps or steps.

There was direct access from the basement into the basement chambers of both the East Tower and the South-East Tower. The East Tower basement was lit by a single loop, but the hexagonal South-East Tower basement has three narrow loops, two of which were cut back so that they could be used as gun-ports. This room was originally vaulted in stone and the wall-ribs, corbels and springers still remain.

THE SOUTH-EAST TOWER

Access to the rooms in the South-East Tower above basement level was by staircase from the ground floor. The hexagonal chambers on all three floors of the tower each contained a garderobe and a fireplace. The ground-floor room above the vaulted basement has three single lancet windows, whilst both upper chambers have two. Access to the southern section of the east curtain wall was down steps within a north-facing doorway from the upper room.

THE SOUTH RANGE

THE GREAT HALL

The Great Hall occupied the eastern part of the South Range. It was a high room, extending to the full height of the curtain wall but, in comparison with Great Halls elsewhere, was not particularly large, measuring 24 feet wide by approximately 40 feet long.

It was entered from the courtyard through an imposing two-centred, arched doorway decorated around the frame with double ogee moulding within a hollow chamfered order. This door originally led into a passageway, the screens passage, of which only the west side survives with its three doorways which gave access to Kitchen, Buttery and Pantry. This arrangement of hall, screens passage and kitchen offices is typical of great medieval houses, and is also found in many Oxford and Cambridge colleges. The screen which separated the screens passage from the Great Hall itself was probably of panelled wood with a gallery over it. There are no surviving traces in either north or south walls of the Hall of screen or gallery, or of a stairway giving access to the gallery.

The cross-wall at the east end of the Great Hall has been destroyed. However, the presence towards

The interior of the South-East Tower; watercolour by S. H. Grimm, 1784 (British Museum)

THE SOUTH RANGE

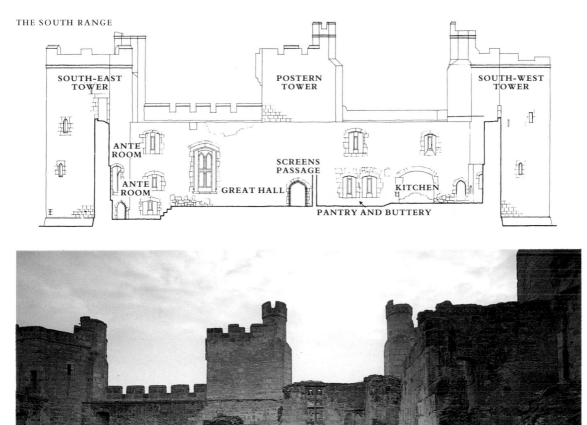

SOUTH-EAST TOWER

POSTERN TOWER

SOUTH-WEST TOWER

ANTE ROOM

ANTE ROOM

GREAT HALL

SCREENS PASSAGE

KITCHEN

PANTRY AND BUTTERY

The South Range: to the left was the Great Hall, to the right the Kitchen

the east end of the curtain wall of a large, transomed window of two pointed lights with stone window seats indicates that the floor level was raised at this end for the dais on which the high table stood. Here Sir Edward Dalyngrigge would have entertained his guests.

The west jamb of at least one further window to light the Great Hall survives in the remaining fragment of courtyard wall to the east of the main doorway. It is most likely that the main fireplace for the room was also in this wall near the dais steps and opposite the window, although it is possible that this room alone could have retained the central fireplace brazier that was traditional before the introduction of chimneys. A doorway led from the Great Hall to the newel staircase, of which only the base survives, in the south-east

This large mullioned and transomed window lit the Great Hall

angle of the courtyard. This staircase provided access to the lord's chambers on the first floor of the East Range.

THE POSTERN TOWER

INTERIOR

The Postern Tower was entered through a door at the south end of the screens passage. Its defences closely resemble those of the main Gatehouse, but are less complex. The gatehouse passage of one bay has a ribbed vault which differs slightly in detail from that of the Gatehouse. The Postern vault rests not on corbels, but on caps and shafts, which are part of the wall structure. The bosses of the vault are pierced with *meurtrières*; the entrance passage was defended by a gate and portcullis at the outer end. There are small, splayed window openings on either side of the passage, and on the west a doorway and newel staircase give access to the floors above.

The chambers on both first and second floors each have a fireplace and garderobe. That on the first floor, the portcullis chamber, has single lancet windows in the south and west faces. The second-floor room has similar windows on south and east faces. Access to the eastern section of the south curtain wall-walk is from this upper chamber.

EXTERIOR

The staircase continues upwards to the roof of the tower, providing access to the parapet. This is projected over the wall faces on corbels and has machicolations pierced in the floor between the corbels in exactly the same way as the Gatehouse defences. The stone crenellations which presumably capped the tower defences are now missing.

On the south face of the tower, between the first- and second-floor windows, are three stone shields in relief. The two outer shields are blank but the middle one bears the coat of arms of Sir Robert Knollys (see Chapter Five), set at an oblique angle and surmounted by a helmet with a ram's head crest.

Beyond the portcullis the gate terminates in a stone bridge abutment with high flanking walls. The floor of this is now solid, but excavations in 1970 demonstrated that it was originally hollow and was bridged. The infilling took place in the seventeenth or eighteenth centuries, perhaps when the castle was dismantled. There are grooves at the south end of both side walls to accommodate an outer gate that may have swung back on to the wall tops, or a drawbridge. The layout of the bridge from this gate to the stone abutment on the south side of the moat is discussed on page 34.

(Opposite page) The Postern Tower

THE KITCHEN RANGE

The rooms of the Kitchen Range, including the Buttery and Pantry, which occupy the western part of the South Range, are less ruinous than those elsewhere; the inner courtyard wall in this corner of the castle still stands to its full height, and gives a good impression of the almost intimate scale and quality of the buildings around the central courtyard.

THE BUTTERY AND PANTRY

The three pointed doorways in the west side of the screens passage gave access to the Buttery and Pantry through the north and south doorways and, through the central, slightly taller doorway, to a passage leading to the Kitchen. The doorways are decorated with hollow chamfers ending in stops. The services of these domestic offices were therefore readily accessible to the Great Hall.

The room adjacent to the courtyard had a small cellar below, lit and ventilated by small openings through to the courtyard. This basement was excavated and partly backfilled by Lord Curzon. The presence of a cellar indicates that the room was probably the Buttery, where ales and wines were

traditionally served. It has two two-light, trefoil-headed windows facing into the courtyard.

The Pantry, on the south side of the kitchen passage, was of a similar plan but without a cellar and with two adjacent single-light windows looking over the moat. It was used for housing kitchen stores.

Above the Buttery and Pantry was a chamber, with a fireplace, of which one jamb survives on the courtyard wall almost immediately above the screen, but no garderobe. Access to it could have been through the minstrels' gallery over the screens passage, although a timber staircase could have been accommodated within the Pantry. There is no connecting doorway with the rooms in the Postern Tower. The room had two tall, double-light transomed windows with trefoiled heads and window seats, of which the western one survives looking into the courtyard, and a single-light window overlooking the moat.

THE KITCHEN

The Kitchen in the south-west corner of the castle, sometimes called the Great Kitchen, was one of the more imposing rooms of the castle, rising two

The ruins of the Kitchen; watercolour by S. H. Grimm, 1784 (British Museum)

The fireplace in the south wall of the Kitchen

storeys in height up to the curtain wall-walk so that the heat of cooking could dissipate. The passage between the Buttery and Pantry provided conveniently direct access to the Great Hall. There was further access from the courtyard through a double-chamfered, four-centred doorway, above which a tall double-light, transomed window with cusped heads extends to almost the full height of the room. The Kitchen was further lit by a single-light window overlooking the moat above the great fireplace in the south wall and a small single-light window in the west wall adjacent to the doorway to the South-West Tower.

The Kitchen has two magnificent fireplaces, in the south and north walls. Both are lined with roof-tiles, laid edge on to prevent cracking in the intense heat. The fireplace in the south wall is 13 feet wide. It had a massive projecting stone hood, now broken, carried on corbels, and a flat bracket on the east side projecting from the top of the jamb, perhaps a sconce for a light. The fireplace on the north side is slightly smaller, and has a circular baking oven set in its west side.

THE SOUTH-WEST TOWER

Two adjacent doorways from the south-west corner of the Kitchen give access into the South-West Tower, which was closely associated with the Kitchen. The northern door leads down from the Kitchen to the castle well in the basement of the tower. The well was discovered and dug out by Curzon. It is 8 feet in diameter and 11 feet deep, lined with dressed stone. Originally fed by a spring, it still contains water. The other doorway opens on a newel stair leading to two hexagonal chambers above the well, both with a fireplace and garderobe, the lower lit by three lancet windows with splayed openings, the upper by two smaller openings, one lancet and one square-headed. The access to the western part of the south curtain wall-walk and the southern part of the western wall-walk is from the upper chamber.

Above these two living-rooms is the castle dovecote or *columbarium*, which was open to the sky and originally contained about 300 nesting boxes, of which 197 survive in stone ledges around the walls.

The well in the South-West Tower

THE WEST RANGE

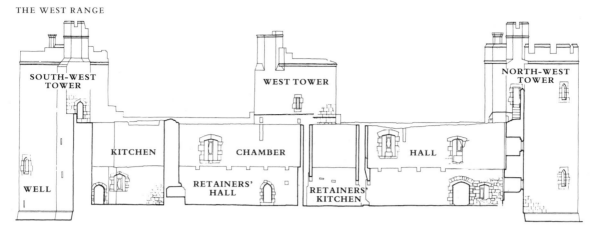

THE WEST AND
NORTH-WEST RANGES

The layout of accommodation within the West
Range and the western part of the North Range
with which it is connected, is difficult to interpret. It
contains a separate kitchen and a number of individual rooms and suites of rooms, which are
generally considered to have been retainers' quarters
and perhaps service rooms. The West and North-
West Towers belong within these suites of rooms.

THE RETAINERS' HALL

At the south end of the West Range a hall on the
ground floor is entered through a double-cham-

fered four-centred arched doorway from the courtyard, but has no direct connection with the 'Great
Kitchen'. The survival of the courtyard wall is
fragmentary but enough remains to reconstruct the
arrangements of windows: two double-light, trefoil-headed windows in square frames and with
stone window seats, of which the south jamb of the
south window survives with the north jamb and
some of the decoration of the north window.

There are no windows in the west wall and the
room must have been fairly dark. There was also no
fireplace, although both the north and south walls
backed on to two substantial fireplaces in the
adjacent kitchens; in the north wall two holes were

The West Range

pierced through the back of the fireplace in the base of the wall, perhaps to increase the draught and to allow heat through.

A doorway in the north wall of the Retainers' Hall led directly into the Retainers' Kitchen. In the south-west corner are slight traces of the scars of a timber staircase which led to the long chamber above.

THE WEST TOWER

A doorway in the west wall of the Retainers' Hall opens on to the spiral staircase which led up to the three levels of small rectangular chambers within the tower. The lower, ground-floor room has no fireplace or garderobe but has three single-light windows. A basement below was entered through a trap door in the floor. The two upper chambers both have fireplaces and garderobes. That on the first floor has two lancet windows, one west- and one north-facing. Access to the northern section of the west curtain wall-walk was from the upper chamber, which has three windows, one facing south, one west and one facing into the courtyard. There is no public access to the upper floor of this tower.

ROOM ABOVE THE RETAINERS' HALL

Above the Retainers' Hall was a further long chamber. It has one single-light window in the west wall, but derived much of its light from the courtyard side, where traces of two tall transomed windows remain. The spacing of these suggests that the original arrangement may have been of three windows. As with the Retainers' Hall below it had no fireplace, again relying on borrowed heat. A doorway in the east side of the north wall leads into an upper gallery or chamber over the adjoining Retainers' Kitchen.

THE RETAINERS' KITCHEN

In the middle of the West Range is a second kitchen, with large fireplaces in both its north and south walls. There was access to this room directly from the courtyard – the south jamb of a double-chamfered doorway survives – and there was also access from the Retainers' Hall. In the south-east corner of the room is a single-light trefoil-headed window opening on to the courtyard at ground-floor level.

On the first floor is the south jamb of a tall transomed window.

The fireplace in the south wall has two holes pierced through to the Retainers' Hall to heat that room. It is a plain undecorated fireplace, with no hood, unlike the main fireplace in the lord's Kitchen. The fireplace in the north wall is of the same shape and is also undecorated, but is now pierced right through the wall into the adjoining chamber. It is probable that it originally had a back, like that in the south wall; the present arrangement is perhaps the result of nineteenth-century repairs.

There is clear evidence for a gallery or a chamber above this kitchen. A doorway leads into it from the first-floor chamber above the Retainers' Hall, and there is the west jamb of a doorway at the east end of the stub of the north wall of the Kitchen. As this room has no west window it must have been lit by windows facing into the courtyard. At ground-floor level the north wall of the kitchen to the east of the fireplace also contains a blocked doorway that would have led to the service rooms and garderobes to the north.

THE NORTH-WEST CORNER AND NORTH-WEST TOWER

It is very difficult now to understand the arrangements of rooms to the north of the Retainers' Kitchen.

There is a slight hint in the arrangement of joist holes for the first floor that a ground-floor partition ran from the south of the double garderobe in the west wall to the inside corner of the courtyard wall. This would suggest a room slightly longer than the Retainers' Kitchen, lit only from the courtyard and heated from the back of the adjacent fireplace in the Retainers' Kitchen. Access was from the courtyard, where the lower jambs of a doorway survive.

Between the corner of the courtyard and the North-West Tower was a further room with a double garderobe recess built into the thickness of the curtain wall near the north end. On either side of the doorway leading into the North-West Tower are two small single-light windows. Access must have been from the room to the south or from that to the east in the North Range.

The North-West Tower

It is likely that there was a partition dividing this room from the ground-floor room in the North Range. This latter was entered from the courtyard, but has no windows in the curtain wall and no fireplace. Again, there were presumably windows on the courtyard side. This bare, austere room must have been a service room of some sort and it has often been suggested that it was perhaps stabling. This may have been so – one would expect provision for horses somewhere within the castle – but Curzon found no traces of internal drains or other features normally associated with stabling and its use must remain an enigma.

At first-floor level there is a hall in the West Range with two small single-light windows in the west wall, of which the northern one has a garderobe opening out from its north jamb. Another small window and a fireplace survive in the north wall; the south end of the room must have been heated by the warmth of the kitchen fireplace chimney within the wall. This room must have been entered from below as there is no access from the North-West Tower at this level.

Access into the first-floor chamber in the North Range could have been from the adjacent first-floor hall in the West Range or from below. There are no external windows and, like the ground-floor rooms, it must have looked out on to the courtyard. There is, however, a fireplace in the north wall, slightly smaller than the fireplace in the adjoining room to the west.

The North-West Tower is entered from the ground floor. There are chambers on three levels, each with a garderobe and fireplace and each with arrangements of two or three single-light lancet windows. From the upper chambers there is access to the western part of the north curtain wall connecting with the Gatehouse. A deep basement beneath the tower must have been entered by a trap-door in the ground floor. The floor of this was 12 feet 6 inches below the floor of the room above and Curzon considered it to be the main dungeon cell of the castle.

THE MUSEUM

Following Lord Curzon's extensive programme of work on the castle, including the digging out of the moat, which took place in 1919, plans were drawn up for a small site museum. The collection was to include a selection of the many objects found during excavations and the paintings, prints and engravings which Lord Curzon had gathered together. A room was added to the existing caretaker's cottage, show cases were made and the museum was opened in 1923. Following Curzon's bequest of the castle to the National Trust in 1926, it was run by a local management committee. In 1931 the executors of Mr W. F. Foster, the first Secretary of the management committee, had a further extension built on to the cottage and museum to house the fine model of the castle built by Mr Foster and the centre-piece of the present display. This was the room in which the museum is now housed and which commands one of the best views of the Gatehouse, providing both a point of reference and a shelter for the visitor in inclement weather.

The show-cases contain a variety of objects including stone and iron shot, and other iron tools and weapons, glass and pottery. The pottery, all fragmentary, ranges in date and style from earthenware cooking and storage vessels of the fourteenth and fifteenth centuries, through post-medieval stoneware vessels, including jugs and tankards, and slip-decorated earthenware, to fine porcelain and china of the last century. The earlier objects derive from the occupants of the castle, the later perhaps from the sumptuous picnics of visitors.

Of particular interest in trying to gain an impression of the decoration of the castle interior are the green and yellow glazed floor-tiles from the Chapel and the fragments of finely carved tracery from the Chapel screen. The alabaster torso of the effigy of a knight is from Robertsbridge Abbey. It is all that remains of the tomb of Sir John Dalyngrigge and is on loan from the Sussex Archaeological Society. The paintings and engravings include works by Lambert, Grimm and the Buck brothers.

CHAPTER SEVEN
THE SETTING

Around the castle there is a complex series of earthworks connected with the construction of the castle moat. The significance of these structures as the remains of landscaped gardens, with water features designed to enhance the castle, has only recently been identified by the Royal Commission on the Historical Monuments of England (RCHME), which considers them to be part of the early landscaping of the castle. Of this remarkable complex only the castle moat survives as a water-filled feature.

The castle is built slightly to the south of the centre of the broad moat, which is rectangular on its west, south and east sides. The broader, more wedge-shaped northern end reflects the northern edge of a string of ponds both to the north-west and to the east. The outlines of these ponds have been mutilated by later drainage and dumping, but are still discernible.

The moat is supplied by a series of springs, a number of which rise from within the moat itself. Others derive from the narrow valley to the north-west of the castle, where there are traces of a pair of tapering ponds retained by a dam across which the

Bodiam from the north-west. The depression in the foreground was once part of a series of ponds that encircled the northern end of the moat

present path runs and from where the original bridge spanned the moat to the Octagon. These ponds had artificially scarped terraces along both their north and south sides, those on the south possibly the line of a carriage-road approach to the castle.

Immediately to the east of the north-east corner of the moat and separated from it by a substantial dam are traces of a further pond with a well-constructed dam along its south side – referred to as the 'Little Moat' on early nineteenth-century maps. There may have been a further pond to the south, separated from the moat by a dam, but its features are now almost obliterated.

To the south and south-west of the castle moat are further complex earthwork features. The most substantial is the large, rectangular hollow between the castle and the present car-park, known since

Plan of the landscaped setting of Bodiam Castle (Royal Commission on the Historical Monuments of England)

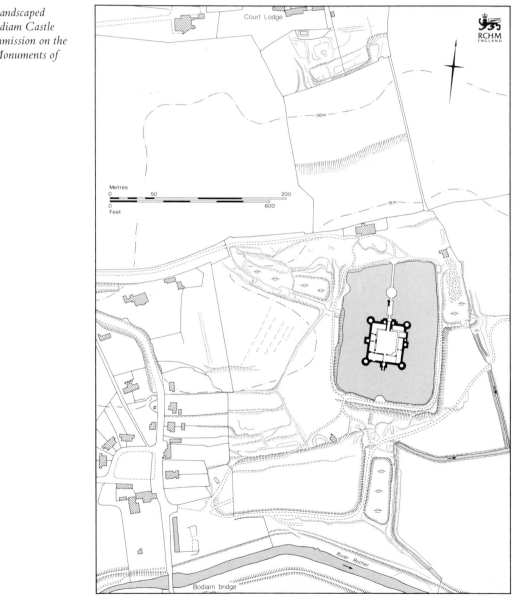

The pillbox to the south of the castle was built during the Second World War as part of the defence of southern England against the threat of German invasion

Curzon's time as the 'Tiltyard'. Indeed, Curzon attempted unsuccessfully to drain it and turn it into a village cricket pitch. However, there can be no doubt that it originally held water and, fed by the leat from 'Dalyngrigge's Bay', served as a header pond for Dalyngrigge's mill, situated somewhere in the vicinity. In the north-east corner of the 'Tilt-yard' is a brick and concrete pillbox erected in 1940 as part of the defence of southern England against the threat of German invasion.

Along the east side of the 'Tiltyard' pond is another quite substantial dam, carrying a footpath along its crest and separating it from a further pond, generally referred to as the 'medieval harbour'. However, as it is above the level of the river, it must always have been a pond, unconnected with the river.

To the north of this pond the rather indeterminate earthworks below the south dam of the moat have been interpreted as the site of the mill, but its presence close to the centre of this carefully contrived landscape and in such a visually prominent position seems unlikely. It has been recently suggested by the RCHME that there may have been a bridge here over a spill-way between the 'Tiltyard' pond and a further small pond to the east.

This seems most likely, if one considers the care taken to stage the views of the castle to visitors approaching from Bodiam Bridge. The path ran along the southern edge of the large, rectangular mill-pond to turn sharply at right angles along the causeway between the mill-pond and the pond to the east. It provided a low, axial view of the battlements of the castle, heightened to dramatic impact upon crossing a bridge and climbing the south dam of the moat. This is one of the most spectacular views of the castle, seen with its reflection in the moat. The continuation of the path along the eastern dam of the moat would have been

between stretches of water and, upon completing the circuit of the moat around its northern bank, the visitor again passed between moat and ponds to reach the long, spectacular bridge across to the Octagon and thence through the Barbican to the Gatehouse. Military considerations aside, this approach would have been impressive and beautiful for visitors with time to appreciate it.

The RCHME has further suggested that the terrace known as the 'Gun Garden' on the hill-slope above the castle to the north would have provided, as a 'Pleasaunce', wonderful views over the land-scaped setting of the castle below. The 'Gun Garden', which stands in the private grounds of the Court Lodge, was partially excavated in the 1960s and shown to have been the site of a medieval building. The terrace, with its buildings, was either originally constructed or later modified to serve as a viewing platform.

Carefully designed landscapes such as this have parallels in the medieval period, but none as early as Bodiam. At Kenilworth Castle in Warwickshire the castle setting is enhanced and defended by a lake, and there is also a 'Pleasaunce', built early in the fifteenth century. In the late sixteenth century at Lyveden in Northamptonshire, areas of water were employed in the unfinished landscape 'garden' and designed for a house which itself was never finished.

Sadly, there are no historical documents which refer to the early setting of the castle, and indeed a paucity of documents for the castle's history generally. However, it seems plausible that the surrounding landscape was constructed by Sir Edward Dalyngrigge as part of his original conception. Such a landscape would certainly have enhanced the castle as a building designed to impress, which combined the most up-to-date military architectural features with comfortable and well-designed accommodation.

APPENDIX

THE LICENCE TO CRENELLATE BODIAM

Rex omnibus ad quos etc. salutem. Sciatis quod de gratia nostra speciali concessimus et licentiam dedimus, quantum in nobis est, dilecto et fideli nostro Edwardo dalyngrigge chivaler, quod ipse mansum manerii sui de Bodyham, juxta mare in comitatu Sussex, muro de petra et calce firmare et kernellare, et castrum inde in defensionem patriae adjacentis et pro resistencia inimicorum nostrorum construere et facere, et mansum predictum sic firmatum et kernellatum et castrum inde sic factum tenere possit sibi et heredibus suis in perpetuum, sine impedimento nostri et heredum nostrorum aut ministrorum nostrorum quoruncunque. In cujus rei testimonium, Rex apud Westmonast. xx die Octobris.

The King to all men to whom etc. greeting. Know that of our special grace we have granted and given license on behalf of ourselves and our heirs, so far as in us lies, to our beloved and faithful Edward Dalyngrigge Knight, that he may strengthen with a wall of stone and lime, and crenellate and may construct and make into a Castle his manor house of Bodyham, near the sea, in the County of Sussex, for the defence of the adjacent country, and the resistance to our enemies, and may hold his aforesaid house so strengthened and crenellated and made into a Castle for himself and his heirs for ever, without let or hindrance of ourselves or our heirs, or of any of our agents whatsoever. In witness of which etc. The King at Westminster 20 October.

Cal. Patent Rolls 1385–9, 42, 123

BIBLIOGRAPHY

GUIDEBOOKS

COTTON, William, *A Graphic and Historical Sketch of Bodyham Castle in Sussex*, London, 1836.

GORHAM, Ticehurst, *Bodiam Castle, Historical and Descriptive*, Battle, 1874.

JOHNSON, Rev. Theodore, *The History of Bodiam, its Ancient Manor, Church and Castle*, Hastings, 1912.

LLOYD, Sir Nathaniel, *Bodiam Castle*, National Trust, c.1938.

MORTON, Catherine, *Bodiam Castle*, Sussex, 1981.

RANGER, William, *A Brief History and Description of Bodiam Castle in Sussex from its Foundation to the Present Day*, Northiam, 1848.

SIMPSON, W. Douglas, *Bodiam Castle, Sussex*, National Trust, 1950.

YARROW, Anne, *Bodiam Castle*, National Trust, 1985.

GENERAL

ALLEN BROWN, R., *English Castles*, Batsford, 1970.

COOPER, William Durrant, 'Pedigree of the Lewknor Family', *Sussex Archaeological Collections*, iii, 1850, pp.89–103.

COULSON, Charles, 'Structural Symbolism in Medieval Castle Architecture', *Journal of the British Archaeological Association*, cxxxii, 1979, pp.72–90.

CURZON OF KEDLESTON, The Marquis, K.G., *Bodiam Castle, A Historical & Descriptive Survey*, Cape, 1926.

CURZON OF KEDLESTON, The Marchioness, G.B.E., *Reminiscences*, Hutchinson, 1955.

DAVIDSON-HOUSTON, Mrs., 'A List of Monumental Brasses in Sussex', *Sussex Archaeological Collections*, lxxvi, 1935, pp.84–7.

DAVISON, Brian, *The Observer's Book of Castles*, Warne, 1979.

FAULKNER, P.A., 'Castle Planning in the Fourteenth Century', *Archaeological Journal*, cxx, 1963, pp.215–3.

GUY, J., *Castles in Sussex, Bodiam*, Phillimore, 1984.

JACKSON-STOPS, G., *The English House in Perspective*, Pavilion, 1990.

JOHNSON, Paul, *The National Trust Book of British Castles*, Cape, 1978.

LEMMON, Lt. Col. Charles H. and DARRELL HILL, J., 'The Romano-British Site at Bodiam', *Sussex Archaeological Collections*, civ, 1966, pp.86–102.

LLOYD, Nathaniel, 'Bodiam Castle', *Journal of the Royal Institute of British Architects*, 1926, pp.442–5.

LOWER, Mark Anthony, 'The Monumental Brasses of Sussex', *Sussex Arch. Colls*, ii, 1849, pp.307–11.

LOWER, Mark Anthony, 'Bodiam and its Lords', *Sussex Arch. Colls*, ix, 1857, pp.274–302.

LOWER, Mark Anthony, 'Notices of Sir Edward Dalygruge, The Builder of Bodiam Castle', *Sussex Arch. Colls*, xii, 1860.

MCLEES, A. David, 'Henry Yevele: Disposer of The King's Works of Masonry', *Journal of the British Archaeological Association*, 1973, pp.52–71.

MARTIN, David, *Report on Excavations at Bodiam Moated Homestead*, Robertsbridge & District Archaeological Society, 1970.

MARTIN, David, *Bodiam Castle. Medieval Bridges*, Hastings Area Archaeological Papers No. 1 (Robertsbridge & District Archaeological Society), 1973.

MYRES, J.N.L., 'The Medieval Pottery at Bodiam Castle', *Sussex Archaeological Collections*, lxxvi, 1935, pp.224–30.

O'NEILL, B.H.St.J., *Castles and Canons*, Clarendon Press, 1960.

PLATT, Colin, *The Castle in Medieval England & Wales*, Secker & Warburg, 1982.

View of Bodiam Castle from the Ewherst Green; water-colour by S. H. Grimm, 1784 (British Museum)

SALZMAN, L.F. & WHISTLER, Hugh, 'Sir John Dalyngrigge & Robertsbridge Abbey', *Sussex Archaeological Collections*, lxxviii, 1940, pp.266–73.

SANDS, Harold, 'Bodiam Castle', *Sussex Archaeological Collections*, xlvi, 1903, pp.112–33.

SAVERY, J.C., 'On Bodiam Manor & Castle', *Journal of the British Archaeological Association*, xxiv, 1868, pp.352–61.

SIMPSON, W. Douglas, 'The Moated Homestead, Church & Castle of Bodiam', *Sussex Archaeological Collections*, lxxii, 1931, pp.68–99.

SMITH, R.D. and BROWN, R.R., 'The Bodiam Mortar', *Journal of the Ordnance Society*, i, 1989, pp.3–22.

THOMAS-STANFORD, Charles, 'The Manor of Radynden: The Radyndens & their successors', *Sussex Archaeological Colls*, lxxii, 1921, pp.64–93.

THOMPSON, M.W., *The Decline of the Castle*, Cambridge University Press, 1987.

TURNER, D.J., 'Bodiam, Sussex: True Castle or Old Soldier's Dream House?', *England in the Fourteenth Century, Proceedings of the 1985 Harlaxton Symposium* in ORMROD W.M. ed., 1986, pp.267–77.

VICTORIA HISTORY OF THE COUNTIES OF ENGLAND, SUSSEX, *Staple Hundred. Bodiam*, 1973, pp.259–65 [reprint of 1937 edition].

WALKER, Simon, 'Lancaster v. Dallingbridge: A Franchisal Dispute in 14th Century Sussex', *Sussex Archaeological Collections*, cxxi, 1983, pp.87–94.

WOOD, Margaret, *The English Medieval House*, 1965.

INDEX

Page numbers in *italic* refer to the illustrations.